See the Dark;

Feel the Light

A poetic journey by
John Den-Kaat

Published by Change Empire Books

© 2022, See the Dark; Feel the Light

Poetry and interior photography by
John Den-Kaat (denkaat@outlook.com)

Cover design by Sara Oliver

ISBN: 978-0-6456902-0-0

Printed in Australia

First Printing, December 2022.

For Dad

As time moves on of course things change.
Our landscape never stays the same.
It's all an impermanent illusion.
Except, my love for you which always remains.

I started writing poetry during a Vipassana silent retreat in 2015, the words just came to me.

I soon came to realise that this me today is not the same me as yesterday or tomorrow or indeed at any time.

I just seek to be the best me I can BE, which is never who I Think I Am (ever).

When I read the insightful thoughts I have had at times I am blown away with their meaning and teachings, and yet I wrote them. These words did not arise from my ordinary mundane brain which fights or entertains my ego but through guidance where my mind and heart meet.

There is a light in everyone and I hope my words help ignite your inner voice.

John Den-Kaat

"When I look inside and see that I'm nothing, that's wisdom. When I look outside and see that I'm everything, that's love. And between these two, my life flows."

Sri Nisargadatta Maharaj

Life is about contrasts and how we navigate them.

This is a poetic expression of a journey into Self.

To see the dark and the shadows we cast and to feel that light within.

As Above, So Below.

The poetry is not mine but for everyone.

This book is for the searcher, the self-discoverer, and those looking for life's meaning or purpose.

Feel with your heart and then you will see.

Contents

Self

"Creepy Friend" (Ego)

What is this feeling I live with day in and out.

Trapped in my body, I want to let it out, but it seems to want to stay.

Every day it creeps around, just showing enough to make me want to respond.

Sometimes I do, sometimes not, either way it will try to get what it wants.

It's okay I say, I know that you are there.

I love you my creepy friend; but I will not feed you today.

Thank you for staying, there is no need to go.

Together we are one and together we will grow.

It harbours the urge to occupy my mind.

By showing its creative talents with pictures and images to protect me from mankind.

I could jump into this imaginary world and act out the illusion

Or I can smile and applaud as audience to its wonderment and deceit.

If I googled its thoughts, the search would be endless.

Be careful of the viruses that are attached underneath.

It is with me now, as I push out these words.

Telling me stories of how I am pitiful and absurd.

I will not judge; it deserves to be here as part of this Act.

I am stronger to know it and I will not react!

Duo

There is two of me inside this shell.

My outer body which cannot tell.

For it is a part of the duo the one not real.

Given life by my thoughts and idolised by how I feel.

The other is my true self which hides deep within.

Mistaken by my choices so I must think again.

Not slave to the process of what life seems to deliver

But nurture and develop the other and
bring it forth to the fore.

Then keep it close to me in the present
everything else is irrelevant.

I take comfort in that insight, now I see
the one that's light,

I cannot know one without the other my
teacher throughout life.

Sit

I feel the pull but resist the urge.

The pull is real the urge is not.

I see the difference and sit with the thought.

Don't push for the former,
just let it flow through your soul.

Surrender all resistance, I AM already Home.

Space

Seize every moment, undenied its current vibe

Breathe into your existence and let
your heart come Alive

Everything is uncertain but this
space that you create

Be still and let awareness guide you
through heaven's gate

Traditional

Being traditional is refreshing, endearing and sweet.

It's not with the norm which bows down at society's feet.

It's being content and being present with
the simplicities of life,

Then expressing your feelings when the pictures not right.

Stay true to your values and love who you are.

Compassionately embrace your individuality
and you will go far.

Walk on the Path "Art"

Art is all around us, it's everywhere we look,

In the nooks and crannies and underneath our foot.

Bring all your senses and imagination and you shall find,

A world of infinite possibilities that is yours and also mine.

Time is of no relevance, just be with all that you uncover.

Art is here in the moment in the familiar or obscure,
be it enemy or lover.

For what you bring to the party is what you will discover.

Look past the obvious and drink in the feelings.

Breathe life into your attention and get drunk
from your very being!

Awe is just Self-Expression of what you out-picture it to be.

It's within these experiences I recognise that
The True work of Art is Me!

Yes

It's not the 'who', 'why' or 'what' but
the inconceivable "YES"!

To let go of all that surpasses and
live life without compromise.

To breathe in every moment or sit back
and watch time unfold.

To know how you are feeling but give in to it anyway.

To dream and be the dreamer,
To love, to dance, to cry, to jump, and touch the sky.

With every moment there resides a gift,
It's yours to keep if you just let it sit.

Be with all that passes because passing it will.
Let it flow through your soul as it sails on its way.

Just a flicker just a pinch is all that it takes, To feel love in this
moment which is with you forever and a day.

Sleep Well

In ignorance I sleep well.

My mind cares not for what ails my internal world.

As I awake in day, now at night.

There is no switch to dampen the beckoning light.

I must listen and be with that voice.

That tells me to act and make the right choice.

So, I can find peace within sleep once again.

Knowing I AM following my spirits life's plan to the end.

Dark

Hamster Wheel

I reach within to find the answers to what the fuck
it's all about.

Am I making the right choices in life because peace seems
still out of sight.

Do we ever truly get there or do we just fleet through this
imaginary existence.

The hamster wheel of life keeps going and going and I
jump off from time to time.

But back on I go even though I see it for what it is.

Let me slow it down and breathe it to a stop.

Then make the right choice so I can forever get off.

Circus

Caught up in this circus of lies and deceit. I see it, I feel it but powerless to defeat.

It is all happening around me, like sheep to the wolves.

No questioning or reasoning; but then who is the Fool?

Despair washes over me; the world has gone bad.

Switch off from the digital echoes that conspires to make me Mad.

Silence and stillness in Truth are the key.

Understand it's an illusion, "I Am" eternally Free.

Love All that surrounds, whether beauty or pain.

Express that knowing outwards, transmute perception again and again.

All is how it should be in this moment it just Is.

The weirder the picture the clearer the internal mist. Like lines in the sand washed away by the waves.

Fleeting images now vanished, only Oneness remains.

Dive Deep

How shallow life is when it's easily disrupted.

A little change is okay but make if too uncomfortable then all Hell gets erupted.

They just take a little, then a little, before tightening the screws.

They want you to comply, so the bastards try to make it unthinkable not to choose.

But when you know it's a lie, you just can't go with the crowd.

Separation gets expanded and critical thinking disallowed.

"How can you be so selfish; look what it's doing to your life."

Take a good look in the mirror;
It's me standing up for what's true and what's right.

Our values should be of the highest, not just lowly material and validated gains.

I will continue to be kind and compassionate but love for our humanity is my aim!

So let it all come and go, I will stay strong and with purpose.

Deep within is my life and I will not swim along with this illusionary Circus.

Cornered

If cornered, I thought I would know what to do.

Well, the walls are closing in and my options are very few.

To make the right choice, living life through my heart,
with an open resolve.

But facing forces out with that keep smothering its call.

Just Trust, I repeat, let go and believe. The answer will come,
Stay eternally Free.

Theatrical Illusion

It's funny ...

The closer we seem to realise our True Self,

The less real becomes the search as it's illusion also melts.

The world that appears it's chaos and decay, it's fragmentation of beliefs and hearsay.

They mean nothing inside not really when we see, All that passes out with is just a smokescreen.

Just a theatrical creation, a projection of our mind.

This room mate who stays hidden and orchestrates our life.

Playing films over and over as our true Self pays the price.

The search is now over, arbitration no more.

I am Home with my creator as I show it the door.

Strangers Smile

A smile from a stranger is all it takes to touch my heart.

Just this fleeting expression leaves a momentary impression

On two souls that know they are not apart.

If we could hold onto that knowing and
keep it with us at all times,

There would be no strangers, just mirrors of ourselves trapped
in this illusionary bind.

The covering of a smile is perhaps one of the greatest crimes.

By covering our face, we separate ourselves from mankind.

So express love how you can, let its energy
touch all in your space.

Keeping faith in your divinity which
has never fallen from Grace.

Non-sense

A sense of Wonder
A sense of Lust
A sense of Anger
A sense of Disgust

They are all the same when their values are removed.

Just Witness their energy before whatever experience ensues.

Release expectation and false preferential circumstance and

Avoid falling into an imaginary external trance.

Your heart is the answer, live there constantly.

Let shifting mind games pass around you and live eternally free.

Shadows in Awareness

Shadows in Awareness are only cues.

That remind "my" soul's impression
is more than what I view.

All is not wasted when seen for what it is.

The fleeting whim of separation deceptively contrasting the
eternal truth that only exists

Look upon every moment not as right or wrong but as passing
contradictions to where "I" belong.

Fear is then redundant, an emotion wrapped in time

Transmute to Love which is always and forever mine.

Dad

Growing up, I'm reminded of how you
would continuously reflect.

I would watch you as your face would give it away, as you fought
your inner egotistical mate.

When you would stare into space during moments of silence,
dissociative fixation on past indiscretions, the world was against
you, and you took the bait.

Casting up insecurities and injustices you
would stew on for days.

Triggering moments of anxiety, fear, and occasional rage.

You were fighting your demons your expressions gave it away.

Dad, you taught me how simple love for your family and
devotion to your wife brought meaning to your life.

Allowing you to escape from what ailed you inside

You never asked for much, just to feel safe and content.

Gentle love to us all is your gift in the end.

Down

At times like these when you're feeling down.

You look around for answers.

The 'where' the 'what' the 'whatever'.

It's funny how I feel comfort in this feeling, this human
condition which doesn't last forever.

I settle into this low vibration with its undertone of emptiness.

I have no thoughts, no distress, and I realise it's for the best.

When you are down you can rise so high and use its foundation
as the catalyst to savour.

As you get back up where you always belonged in the loving
arms of your maker.

Light

At the Precipice

Standing at the precipice; no point in Time.

No point in doing, just Being in Kind.

No need for answers when all questions have dissolved

Just feeling the way with Love, letting that next step be "All".

No-things Wasted

Could you throw the first stone. Catch a falling star.

Breathe life into your being or Daydream the path so far.

Run rings around your neighbours and
laugh behind their back or

Give charity to a stranger and expect nothing back.

Sit silently in a crowded room and pretend
you're wearing a mask or

Stand upright on your soap box and never be brought to task.

It's all as it is.

Nothings wasted, all part of the Whole.

Don't sweat past situations, come Home and Free your Soul

All is Past

What's in front of me has already passed.

My senses just transmuted, and my mind has just grasped.

In truth let it be, let the experience feel free.

Give it awareness give it light but don't get uptight.

To prefer something different, is imagining; not real

By putting Me in the picture can produce an illusionary feel.

I am not what is happening but the observer that's all.

One with the Devine Essence whom created us whole.

Oh, Nothing

Ours is not to reason what is wrong or right.

Just flow with the current and take nothing at first sight.

Reflect not deflect the tribulations of life.

Everything is a beginning, let go, let your dreams take flight.

Nothing is easy, but then nothing is Real.

Once you grab this concept, you can never ever fail.

All that has come before I honour and warmly embrace.

My journey made possibly by everyone I invited on this stage.

Thank you for this gift, my existence Here.
Where nothing is ever wasted, and everything is "clear"

Knock and Surrender

The bravado of life takes on many forms.

The intrinsic details in its fabric can only be
realised away from the norm.

Our staged box of "self" is undulating not static or fixed.

Escape from its containment and fake clutches
of struggles and strife.

Keep knocking on its walls to reveal crevices of light.

Then with courage, extend and reach into this unknown.

Find strength from vulnerability and the
freedom of just letting go.

Surrender

The universe will deliver if you just let all things be.

Trust and allow joy in your heart and see where it may lead.

Be grateful for all life's beauty, as it is always here.

At times of despair amazing gifts will appear.

They will happen at just the right time to light your way.

Stay open to receive them and let Love guide your day.

The Path to Remember

As I strive for meaning within this illusionary existence.

Are my intentions Pure or fuelled by my ego's persistence?

What is my purpose, what is my Path?

Give me some guidance, give me some a-has!

To search is perhaps nonsensical, there is no agenda.

The path does not lead anywhere; it is a path to Remember.

"All that there is" is here in this Moment

BEING aware of our Oneness leads to the Atonement.

Be forgiving, be open hearted and let Love light the way.

Then willingly remember the Truth;
I am Home and I've never been away

Boomerang

The Boomerang of Love has no bounds
I release mine out without grounds

It reverberates throughout this illusionary plane
touching sleepy souls resonating again and again

Then returns to me stronger than before
opening up my heart centre to help me remember

Before taking flight again without any agenda

Conductor

With space and distance my heart gets fuller. The love it
absorbs has never been truer.

It reveals my true self, the light in the shadow,
As it shines within me I remember to honour,
This present day where I am the conductor.

Let me orchestrate outward that which my heart does teach,
As we make music together and dance to Loves beat.

Don't question each moment let it be as it is.
The miracle that is us, a life of Pure Bliss.

Where the Heart and the Mind Meet.

The Heart reflects upon itself touching
the calm waters of the Mind.

It sees within itself and gives Light to the insight of the Soul.

.